Zia Blizz

FAMILY SAFE SITUATIONS GET TO KNOW THEM

Situations to play Platonically

Family Safe Situations from Truth, Dare & Situations

First Published in **December 2024**

ISBN: 978-93-6356-392-6

PUBLISHING MONGERS

+91 9311101365

Distributed by: Watergies

Rules of engagement

- Minimum players : 2; Maximum players : 10; Best played with : 4-5

- With 2 players, you choose either his team or her team, and ask whatever your team gets. You can both answer the same questions too, if mutually decided, or start over from the other's team

- With more than 2 players, everyone answers every question

- Every player gets to skip a maximum of three answers to questions. NO EXCEPTIONS.

- Go, get to know them without the risk of going too far

Her turn

#1

If you could talk
to one person
from history,
who would you
talk to

His turn

#2

If you could ask God one question, what would it be

Her turn

#3

If you could make one person's wish come true, who would you ask

His turn

#4

If you could rain
food, what would
you want to rain

#5

If you could travel anywhere, where would you go

#6

If you found a genie that grants you three wishes, what would you wish

Her turn

#7

If you could become a dog, what breed would you want to be

#8

If you could live forever, what would you do differently

#9

If you could live in any country in the world, where would you live

His turn

#10

If you could swap lives with me for a day, what would you do as me

#11

If you could watch only one streaming service, which would you

#12

If someone left you a house in their will, where would you want it to be

Her turn

#13

If you lost your
passport on
vacation, what
would you do

His turn

#14

If you find a suitcase in the woods with a million bucks, would you take it

#15

If you woke
tomorrow to be
thirteen again,
what would you
do

His turn

#16

If you could choose what age to die at, what would you choose

#17

If you woke up
tomorrow and
your entire life
was a dream, how
would you react

His turn

#18

If you were a villainous scientist, what would you invent

Her turn

#19

If you could see one hour into the future constantly, how would you use it

His turn

#20

If you wanted the perfect proposal, how would you want it

Her turn

#21

If you bumped into a parked car, would you leave your details

His turn

#22

If you could solve a historical mystery, which one would you choose

Her turn

#23

If you were a dictator of a small country, what would you do

His turn

#24

If you have to
award the best
invention ever,
what would it be

Her turn

#25

If time machines
existed, what
would be the
first thing you
would do

His turn

#26

If you can create another season of a show, which show would you choose

Her turn

#27

If a friend calls to bury a body, what would you do

His turn

#28

If your house had a theme song, what would it be

Her turn

#29

If you could relive a memory, which would you choose

His turn

#30

If your ten year old self wrote your profile, what would it say

Her turn

#31

If you had could change one thing about your life, what would you change

His turn

#32

If you could choose between being a ghost or find out afterlife, what would you choose

#33

If you could
have a mentor,
who would you
choose

His turn

#34

If you could
abolish a law,
what would it be

Her turn

#35

If you were the ruler of the world and could make one rule, what would it be

His turn

#36

If you could learn any skill you want in the world immediately, which one would you learn

Her turn

#37

If you could return
to Earth as
anything other
than a human,
what would you
choose

#38

If you could
unlimited supply
of one thing,
which would you
choose

#39

If you could be the CEO of any company, which would you choose

His turn

#40

If you could
never get sick,
would you
sacrifice a finger
for it

Her turn

#41

If you could make people believe that anything is possible, what would you make them believe

His turn

#42

If you had to
pick somewhere
in history to live
in, when would
you live

Her turn

#43

If you could eat only one food for the rest of your life, what would it be

His turn

#44

If you could live for five hundred years, what would you do differently

Her turn

#45

If only one book
existed, which
book would you
like it to be

His turn

#46

If you could kill anyone in history, who would you kill

Her turn

#47

If you could
choose one
career for me,
what would it be

#48

If you could
make a band
with three
artists, who
would you choose

Her turn

#49

If you could build your dream home, what would it be like

#50

If you had to choose a last meal, what would it be

Her turn

#51

If you had a
theme song,
what would it be

#52

If you could ask
one question to
your future self,
what would it be

Her turn

#53

If you travel to another world being frozen for a hundred years, would you

His turn

#54

If you could read minds, what would you do

Her turn

#55

If you had to live
in jail forever or
die right now,
what would you
choose

#56

If we were stuck
on a deserted
island, what
three items
would you bring

Her turn

#57

If you could un-invent something, what would you choose

#58

If we could throw a party with unlimited budgets, what all would you do

#59

If you could be
a character in
any book, who
would you be

#60

If you start reading a book that is your life, would you read it till the end

#61

If you could pick
one movie to
become your life,
which would you
choose

His turn

#62

If you could see
the future, what
would you do

Her turn

#63

If you child
wanted to drop
out and start a
business, how
would you react

His turn

#64

If your child wanted to get married in school, how would you react

Her turn

#65

If you could eat
food forever
without gaining
weight, what
would you choose

#66

If we could be characters in a movie, which would you choose

Her turn

#67

If animals could talk, would you still eat them

#68

If you were of the opposite gender, how would your life be different

Her turn

#69

If you could choose an age to be again, which would you choose

#70

If you could travel to the future at your own funeral, would you want to

Her turn

#71

If you were
going to go blind
in one week,
what would you
want to see

His turn

#72

If you could live as super rich in a third world country, would you

Her turn

#73

If you had to choose between permanent day or permanent night, which would you choose

His turn

#74

If you had the choice never sleep, would you do it

Her turn

#75

If you can live in
a castle, which
one would it be

#76

If you could change evolution, what would you change

Her turn

#77

If you have an extra hour everyday while the world sleeps, what would you do

His turn

#78

If you went deaf but you can memorise one sound, what would you choose

Her turn

#79

If we had a whole
day to ourselves
with no
responsibilities,
what would you
want to do

His turn

#80

If you could fly,
what would you
do

#81

If you could live in a fictional world, which would you choose

His turn

#82

If you erase one vegetable, which would you choose

Her turn

#83

If you could do
one thing without
repercussions,
what would you
do

#84

If you were the last person on Earth, what would you do

Her turn

#85

If you could ask me any question that I would answer honestly, what would it be

His turn

#86

If you were
going to die, who
would be your
last call

Her turn

#87

If you could
eliminate all
diseases, would
you kill a child
for it

His turn

#88

If you could be
one age forever,
what age would
you choose

Her turn

#89

If you know
someone is
coming to kill
you, what would
you do

#90

If you could get a new thing everyday starting with a single letter, which letter would you choose

Her turn

#91

If you could stop time, what would you do

His turn

#92

If you had to
disappear, how
would you do it

Her turn

#93

If we could start a business together, what would it be

His turn

#94

If you could watch only one movie forever, which would you choose

#95

If you could destroy one planet, which would you choose

His turn

#96

If you find out
you were
adopted, what
would you do

Her turn

#97

If your phone
fell in the toilet,
what would you
do

His turn

#98

If you could
have any wish
fulfilled, what
would you wish

#99

If you won the
lottery
tomorrow, what
would you do

#100

If we could share memories, what would you like me to see

Her turn

Bonus

Something you want her to imagine

His turn

Bonus

Something you want him to imagine